A
WORLD
FULL
OF
POEMS

SELECTED BY
SYLVIA M. VARDELL

ILLUSTRATED BY
SONNY ROSS

Project Editor Abby Aitcheson
Senior Editor Jolyon Goddard
Designer Sonny Flynn
Senior Art Editor Rachael Parfitt Hunt
Managing Editor Jonathan Melmoth
Managing Art Editor Diane Peyton Jones
US Editor Margaret Parrish
US Senior Editor Shannon Beatty
Producer, Pre-Production Abi Maxwell
Production Controller Basia Ossowska
Jacket Designer Sonny Flynn
Jacket Co-ordinator Issy Walsh
Publishing Director Sarah Larter

First American Edition, 2020
Published in the United States by DK Publishing
1450 Broadway, Suite 801, New York, NY 10018

Poems copyright © the individual poets
The acknowledgments on page 204 constitute
an extension of this copyright page

Copyright © 2020 Dorling Kindersley Limited
DK, a Division of Penguin Random House LLC
22 23 24 10 9 8 7 6 5 4
006-316752-Oct/2020

A catalog record for this book
is available from the Library of Congress.
ISBN 978-1-4654-9229-6

DK books are available at special discounts when purchased
in bulk for sales promotions, premiums, fund-raising, or
educational use. For details, contact: DK Publishing Special
Markets, 1450 Broadway, Suite 801, New York, NY 10018
SpecialSales@dk.com

Printed and bound in China

For the curious

www.dk.com

CONTENTS

ANIMALS AND NATURE

CITIES, TOWNS, AND TRAVEL

FUN AND GAMES

SCIENCE AND ART

BODY AND HEALTH

A WORLD OF LEARNING

The poems in this book are presented in exactly the same way as the poets wrote them, including their spelling, punctuation, capitalization, spacing, and indentation.

INTRODUCTION

by Sylvia Vardell

Welcome to a world full of poems—full of rhyme and rhythm, emotion and imagination; poems about everything from friends and families to feet and fish rain, written by poets from around the world. Share a poem out loud with a friend or read a poem quietly alone. Start from the beginning or flip to a surprise page. There are poems here for everyone—humorous, serious, short, long, familiar, or brand-new. Plus, you'll find activities in the back to help you think, draw, write, and share. Let's get started!

Sylvia Vardell is an award-winning professor at Texas Woman's University and the author of many books and articles about children's literature, poetry for children, and teaching.

Sonny Ross is an illustrator based in Manchester, UK. He uses skills gained from editorial illustration to inform his children's book work. He also has two cats that are plotting against him.

FAMILY
AND FRIENDS

For many of us, life is all about family and friends.
Poetry helps us explore these different
human relationships.

New Baby

Ralph Fletcher

Soon as the baby gets born
before she's two hours old
people start dividing her up.

"She has Daddy's big ears"
"Got Grandma's double chin"
"She has my olive eyes"

like she's just a bunch
of borrowed parts
stitched together.

Well, I just got to hold her.
I touched her perfect head
and I'll tell you this:

My sister is whole.

What Will You Choose, Baby?

Linda Sue Park

Pen for writer.
Book for teacher.
Bowl of rice keeps hunger at bay.

Coins mean riches,
Thread, long life.
Cakes for the greedy—push them away!

Mama's laughter,
Daddy's camera.
Grandpa, Grandma, clap and cheer.

Hugs abounding.
Love surrounding.
Celebration! Your first year!

Note: On a Korean baby's first birthday, many families play the "fortune game." Objects symbolizing various futures are placed in front of the baby: whatever the baby chooses is said to predict its future.

I'm Bigger

Kristy Dempsey

You wobble.
I walk.
You babble.
I talk.
You sit
and drool
and swing,
while I draw
and dance
and sing.
I can say my ABCs.
You just jiggle
plastic keys.
I can run
and jump
and spin …

and when I do,
it makes you grin.
I am bigger.
You're so small.
(But I still love you
best of all.)

Happy Adoption Day

Jane Yolen

This is the day we celebrate
Adoption Day, our family date,
The day that in that faraway year
I traveled from where I was to here.

By bus, by plane, by train, by car.
I carried my heart so very far
To find my place, to find my home,
The people I could call my own.

So on this day, let's all agree
To celebrate not only me,
But family.

Double the Trouble

Janet Wong

My family
is made up of

two mothers,
two fathers,
two sisters,
two brothers,
two dogs,
and two cats
in two
different houses

with double
the shopping
and double
the laundry
and double
the trouble
and double
the noise—

and twice as much
love for us
girls and us boys.

Three

Chrissie Gittins

My best friend has a best friend,
she is a bester friend than me,
but when they have a falling out
my friend is best with me.

At Our House

Virginia Euwer Wolff

Dad reads to me while he makes me lunch,
Mom reads to me in bed.
My little brother wants to hear
every word that we have read.

Grandpa's learning how to read,
Grandma hums along.
Books speak right up in our house,
and words turn into song.

Abuelita

Margarita Engle

We called her little grandmother
even though she was big.

Her house was small
and the street was muddy.
Her neighbors rode horses
and lived in thatched huts.
She believed in the goodness
of ladylike manners.
She taught me how to embroider
a garden,
decorating the world
with a sharp needle,
one flowery stitch
at a time.

Note: *Abuelita* is a Spanish term of affection for a
grandmother, similar to "grandma" or "granny."

A Suitcase of Seaweed

Janet Wong

Across the ocean
from Korea
my grandmother,
my Halmoni,
has come—
her suitcase
sealed shut
with tape,
packed full
of sheets
of shiny black
seaweed
and stacks
of dried squid.

We break it open,
this old treasure
chest of hers,
holding
our noses
tight
as we release
its ripe
sea smell.

Our Blended Family

Doraine Bennett

patchwork family
stitched together
by threads of love
a crazy quilt
of unexpected color

Granny's Teapots

Michelle Schaub

So prim and proper,
they perch atop cabinets,
adorned in party dresses.
Roses,
pinstripes,
polka dots.
Some tall and thin,
some short and squat.
All pose,
one arm akimbo,
the other pointing high—
waiting,
patient,
while I choose:
Which will host
our tea for two?

Something I Did

Janet Wong

Something I did
made Alex
not like me.
Something I did—
but what?
If Alex would tell me,
if Alex would say—
then maybe
we'd fix things
and
we could play
together
at recess
like we used to do.
What did I do wrong?
I wish I knew.

Dad

Andrew Fusek Peters

He's a:

Tall story weaver
Full of fib fever
Bad joke teller
Ten decibel yeller
Baggy clothes wearer
Pocket money bearer
Nightmare banisher
Hurt heart vanisher

Bear hugger
Biscuit mugger
Worry squasher
Noisy nosher
Lawn mower
Smile sower

Football mad
Fashion sad
Not half bad
So glad I had
My
Dad!

A Day to Honor Fathers

Carole Gerber

Papá, Vader, Babbo, Tad.
Babba, Otac, Apa, Dad.

Tatti, Tata, Tevs, and *Appa.*
Pita-ji, Daidl Isa, Bapa.

Around the world, we children say,
Thank you! Happy Father's Day!

Louder than a Clap of Thunder!

Jack Prelutsky

Louder than a clap of thunder,
louder than an eagle screams,
louder than a dragon blunders,
or a dozen football teams,
louder than a four-alarmer
or a rushing waterfall,
louder than a knight in armor
jumping from a ten-foot wall.

Louder than an earthquake rumbles
louder than a tidal wave,
louder than an ogre grumbles.
as he stumbles through his cave,
louder than stampeding cattle,
louder than a cannon roars,
louder than a giant's rattle
that's how loud my father *SNORES!*

Sincerely

Robyn Hood Black

Dear Friend,

I see the thoughtful things you do.
Your words are always cheerful, too.

I noticed!
And I'm thanking you.

Sincerely,
Me

How to Make a Friend

Jane Heitman Healy

You start by saying *Hi there,*
Hello, Aloha, Ciao—
If someone answers back to you,
Smile and nod and bow.

You might try saying *Hola,*
Salut, Goddag, Shalom.
If someone answers back to you,
They might be far from home.

A friend begins by greeting
Those they meet along the way
To make them feel welcome
At home, at school, at play.

Friend

Philip Waddell

Arm linker
Eye winker
Time sparer
Treat sharer.

Hand lender
Defender
Word taker
Peacemaker.

Work keeper
Praise heaper
High fiver
Reviver.

Compliment Chain

Mary Lee Hahn

Your two small words
Good job!
filled me up
I sat straighter in my chair.
I *had* worked hard.
And you noticed.

My friend
is bent over his paper.
His pencil moves slowly, carefully.
I say two small words,
Good job!
And watch him sit up straight.

Friends

Renée M. LaTulippe

Annie

has a chair on wheels.

She's fast

and she can spin!

We race each other

after school.

Sometimes she lets me win.

Robert

doesn't talk like me,

but draws

a whole lot better.

He points out pictures

in our books,

and I point out each letter.

Lucy
moves her hands to speak,
her fingers
forming shapes.
We are silent
superheroes
in our masks and capes.

My friends and I
are different,
but not in every way.
All of us love having fun—
we read
and draw
and play!

FEELINGS

Poets have a gift for capturing all the different emotions we feel—happiness, fear, anger, loneliness, gratitude, frustration, and more.

A Way Around

Naomi Shihab Nye

Argument
is a room I won't enter.
Some of us
would circle a whole house
not to enter it.

If you want to talk like that,
try a tree.
A tree is patient.
Don't try me.

Alone

Ros Asquith

I want to be alone today,
I want to be alone.
I want to be alone, I say,
That means, be on my own.

I'm talking to myself today
(I really hope you'll keep away).
Sometimes it is the only way
to find just what I want to say.

I need to be alone.

Anger

John Foster

Anger
Is a red bull
Charging through the mind's fields,
Inciting actions you may soon
Regret.

Pout

Sara Holbrook

No use
acting nice to me
when I'm stuck
in a pout.
I can't let your
niceness in
until my mad
wears
out.

I'm Nobody! Who Are You?

Emily Dickinson

I'm nobody! Who are you?
Are you nobody, too?
Then there's a pair of us – don't tell!
They'd banish us, you know.

How dreary to be somebody!
How public, like a frog
To tell your name the livelong day
To an admiring bog!

Question

Ros Asquith

If we had everything we want –
the music, toys, the food,
perfect schools, perfect dads,
all things easy and good.
And none of the things we don't want –
no worries, anguish, fuss.
No mad days, bad days, sad days –
would we still be us?

I Woke Up This Morning

Karla Kuskin

I woke up this morning
at quarter past seven.
I kicked up the covers
and stuck out my toe.
And ever since then
(that's a quarter past seven)
they haven't said anything
other than "no."
They haven't said anything
other than "Please, dear,
don't do what you're doing,"
or "Lower your voice."
Whatever I've done
and however I've chosen,
I've done the wrong thing
and I've made the wrong choice.

I didn't wash well
and I didn't say thank you.
I didn't shake hands
and I didn't say please.
I didn't say sorry
when passing the candy
I banged the box into
Miss Witelson's knees.
I didn't say sorry.
I didn't stand straighter.
I didn't speak louder
when asked what I'd said.
Well, I said
that tomorrow
at quarter past seven
they can
come in and get me.
I'm Staying In Bed.

Me in a Tree

Julie O'Callaghan

Unfortunately, it wasn't
a luxury tree house
with hot and cold running cocoa
or with a robin

bringing me breakfast in bed.
A squirrel didn't toss acorns
at me when I needed to wake up.
No – that wasn't how it was.

I hid high up in the leaves.
So many thoughts were floating,
I speared them on to twigs
to see them twinkle in the sun.

But now I realise
I named this poem the wrong thing.
It's not me in a tree.
It's the tree in me.

Poem for a Bully

Eileen Spinelli

Somewhere deep inside you
there's a softer, kinder place.
I know this will surprise you—
but I've seen it in your face.
Your eyes are often sad, although
you wear a surly grin.
Sometimes when you stand all alone
your "mean" seems worn and thin.
I wish that you would take a step—
a small but brave one, too—
and look inside yourself to find
the good I see in you.

When I'm Angry

Brenda Williams

I'm a
Huff taker
Quarrel maker

Face scowler
Voice growler

Help resenter
Friendship denter

Pencil snapper
Finger tapper

Game spoiler
Blood boiler

Foot stamper
Mouth clamper

Cushion whammer
Door slammer

Book thrower
Steam blower

Bed flopper
Tear dropper

Calm taker
Peace maker

I Wish I Had More Courage

Toon Tellegen

I WISH I had more courage.

  I've got so little of it…

  If courage was something you could buy,

  I'd spend all my money on it.

  It would be my most valuable possession.

  Ordinary courage. Not heroism or recklessness.

  Everyday courage.

  People would talk about me like this:

  "See that kid there?"

  "Yes."

  "Do you know what he is?"

  "No."

  "Brave. Very brave."

  "Really?"

  "Yes, really."

  Then I'd get happiness too at no extra cost.

Translated by David Colmer

44

Don't Be Scared

Carol Ann Duffy

The dark is only a blanket
for the moon to put on her bed.

The dark is a private cinema
for the movie dreams in your head.

The dark is a little black dress
to show off the sequin stars.

The dark is the wooden hole
behind the strings of happy guitars.

The dark is a jeweller's velvet cloth
where children sleep like pearls.

The dark is a spool of film
to photograph boys and girls,

so smile in your sleep in the dark.
Don't be scared.

Rush – Jesse

Nikki Grimes

Buck up! Be brave!
Get over it!
Those words make me
just want to spit.

Folks wind my sadness
like a clock.
"Time's up," they say.
Tick tock, tick tock.

"Forget your tears.
You've cried enough.
You've lost someone.
We know that's tough,

but now it's time
to move along."
They're telling me
my heart is wrong

for hurting past
the date they set?
Well, I'm not ready
to move on yet.

Lost

Kate Coombs

I lost a friend today.

I said some words
no one should say.

I watched her face change,
and then

I watched her walk
away.

Look for the Helpers

Michelle Heidenrich Barnes

Look for the helpers
The healers
The givers

The arms-open
Hand-holding
Everyday heroes

The ones who bring food
Extra clothes
And first aid

Who offer safe shelter
A roof
And a bed

Follow their lead
Be a hugger
A helper

A friend who will listen
A person
Who cares

Too Shy

Linda Kulp Trout

Tonight
I watched
a harvest moon
tiptoe
across the sky.
It hid behind
a wisp of clouds,
looking very
shy.

I said,
Don't worry
Harvest Moon,
for I'm a lot
like you.
When I'm feeling
shaky, shy—
I try
to hide it
too.

How to Love Your Little Corner of the World

Eileen Spinelli

Help a neighbor.
Plant a tree.
Hug your friends
and family.
Be kind to pets.
Feed the birds.
Use your *please*
and *thank you* words.
Share a book.
Take a walk.
Someone's lonely?
Stop and talk.

A Happy Kenning

Clare Bevan

It's a...
Face-Quaker,
Head-Shaker,
Chin-Jiggler
Body-Wriggler,
Knee-Slapper,
Hand-Flapper,
Eye-Mopper,
Tantrum-Stopper,
Frown-Cheater,
Gloom-Beater,
Ice-Breaker,
Friend-Maker,
Mood-Shifter,
Spirit-Lifter,
Joy-Bringer,
Heart-Singer,
LAUGH!

Note: "Kenning" means making up a term using two nouns to describe something, often metaphorically, as used in this poem.

Although

Tony Langham

Although
I had

butterflies
in my
stomach

and ants
in my pants

and a bee
in my
bonnet

and a flea
in my
ear —

I had
a whale
of a time.

ANIMALS AND NATURE

Our world is full of fascinating features and incredible creatures. Poems can show us details that we may never have noticed before.

Petting Zoo

Laura Purdie Salas

Bossy goats,
Floppy dogs,
Silky bunnies,
Bristly hogs.

Milk a cow,
Find a nest.
I like cuddling
Kittens best!

At the Zoo

William Makepeace Thackeray

First I saw the white bear, then I saw the black;

Then I saw the camel with a hump upon his back;

Then I saw the grey wolf, with mutton in his maw;

Then I saw the wombat waddle in the straw;

Then I saw the elephant a-waving of his trunk;

Then I saw the monkeys—mercy, how unpleasantly they smelt!

Animal Talk

Charles Ghigna

Ducks quack
Doves coo
Dogs bark
Cows moo

Birds sing
Bears growl
Bees buzz
Wolves howl

Geese honk
Gulls cry
Cats mew
Guess why

Mice squeak
Mules bray
Animals have
Something to say!

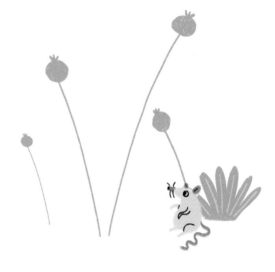

Watch Your Step

Leslie Bulion

It's a bug's world of intrigue and mystery,
with humans a blip in their history.
So when insects flitter and scurry past us
Take note, because they may outlast us!

Zoophabet: Ants to Zorillas

Avis Harley

Ants use antennae to seek out their tracks,

Beavers gnaw trees for their lodge,

Camels store food in the humps on their backs,

Dragonflies dazzle and dodge,

Elephant trunks furnish watery flings,

Flamingoes eat shrimp to keep pink;

Grasshoppers' ears appear under their wings,

Hummingbirds hover to drink,

Inchworms advance with a rear-ended loop,

Jellyfish sometimes can sting,

Kestrels catch lunch with a lightning-like swoop,

Larks love to warble and sing,

Moles tunnel intricate malls underground,

Newts thrive in ponds filled with weed,

Owls like to swivel their heads right around,

People can learn how to read,

Quetzals are gorgeous in feathery dress,

Rats have acquired a bad label,

Seahorse appears like a figure in chess,

Tortoise found fame in a fable,

Umber-birds thrive in the African wild,

Vipers can poison their prey,

Worms turn the soil when the climate is mild,

Xylophage chews wood all day,

Yaks grow in horns that are gracefully curled,

Zorillas are striped black and white;

      each zooabet creature is part of this world:

      unique, with its own copyright!

Let's Celebrate the Elephant

Irene Latham

What other animal

has a dump truck body
stuck on tree stump feet?

I like the way its skin
comes in shades of concrete.

See its hosepipe trunk
and sailboat ears?

Its tail is a windshield wiper
for its rear.

Eletelephony

Laura Elizabeth Richards

Once there was an elephant,
Who tried to use the telephant—
No! No! I mean an elephone
Who tried to use the telephone—
(Dear me! I am not certain quite
That even now I've got it right.)
Howe'er it was, he got his trunk
Entangled in the telephunk;
The more he tried to get it free,
The louder buzzed the telephee—
(I fear I'd better drop the song
Of elephop and telephong!)

The Crocodile

Lewis Carroll

How doth the little crocodile
Improve his shining tail,
And pour the waters of the Nile
On every golden scale!

How cheerfully he seems to grin,
How neatly spreads his claws,
And welcomes little fishes in,
With gently smiling jaws!

Dressing
Like a Snake

Georgia Heard

A snake changes its clothes
only twice a year.
Beginning with its nose,
peeling down to its toes:
new clothes suddenly appear.
Wouldn't it be nice
to dress only twice
instead of each day of the year?

Trust

Padma Venkatraman

My cat
hissed and spat
at the vet. "I'll help,"
I said. She squirmed and yelped
when I held her tight.

To calm her fright
I kissed her head
and whispered soothing words.

She
licked me
with her ticklish tongue.

Her grass-green eyes
gazed into mine.
"You'll be fine,"
I promised,

feeling like my mommy
must have felt,
holding squalling baby
me,
when we visited a doctor.

April Is a Dog's Dream

Marilyn Singer

april is a dog's dream

the soft grass is growing

the sweet breeze is blowing

the air all full of singing feels just right

so no excuses now

we're going to the park

to chase and charge and chew

and I will make you see

what spring is all about

The Moon

Robert Louis Stevenson

The moon has a face like the clock in the hall;
She shines on thieves on the garden wall,
On streets and fields and harbour quays,
And birdies asleep in the forks of the trees.

The squalling cat and the squeaking mouse,
The howling dog by the door of the house,
The bat that lies in bed at noon,
All love to be out by the light of the moon.

But all of the things that belong to the day
Cuddle to sleep to be out of her way;
And flowers and children close their eyes
Till up in the morning the sun shall arise.

When the Rain Falls

Susan Taylor Brown

Clouds curl.
Thunder trembles.
Lightning leaps.
Coats cover.
Umbrellas unfold.
Wipers wave.
Rivers rise.
Buckets bail.
Puddles plash.
Mud melts.
Worms wiggle.
Rainbows reappear.

An Autumn Greeting

George Cooper

"Come," said the Wind to the Leaves one day.
"Come over the meadow and we will play.
Put on your dresses of red and gold.
For summer is gone and the days grow cold."

The Best Paths

Kristine O'Connell George

The best paths
are whispers
in the grass,
a bent twig,
a token, a hint,
easily missed.

The best paths
hide themselves
until the right
someone
comes along.

The best paths
lead you
to where
you didn't know
you wanted to go.

Clouds

Kate Coombs

I saw one little cloud
that looked like a wish,
but now there's a crowd
like a school of white fish.

Clouds can turn red at sunset
or shine with gold light.
Sometimes dark clouds growl
with thunder at night.

There are clouds flat as paper
and clouds fat as geese,
clouds built like staircases,
clouds soft as fleece.

But clouds *should* look wet—
and do you know why?
All clouds are secretly
lakes in the sky.

Fish Rain

Marilyn Nelson

Animal rain is an extremely rare
meteorological phenomenon.
Once in a weird while, it rains animals.
Not cats and dogs, but toads and frogs, always
the same species, and always the same size.
The most rained animals are tiny fish.
What makes live fish fall out of thunderclouds
many miles away from the nearest lake?
Are they whooshed up by fierce tornadic winds?

It has rained fish in Australia, India,
Louisiana, and Saskatchewan.
And in Yoro, a town in Honduras,
fish rain falls one or two times every year.
They celebrate it with a festival
thanking the fish rain for feeding the poor.
You'll probably never walk in a fish rain.
But, just in case, remember if you do,
to carry your umbrella upside down!

Who Has Seen the Wind?

Christina Rossetti

Who has seen the wind?
Neither I nor you:
But when the leaves hang trembling,
The wind is passing through.

Who has seen the wind?
Neither you nor I:
But when the trees bow down their heads,
The wind is passing by.

Summer Storm

Irene Latham

Cloud warns, *get ready.*
Lightning spits, *all clear.*
Thunder growls, *Hello, Dog.*
Dog yips, *get out of here!*

Rain roars, *is that all you've got?*
Dog whimpers, *go away.*
Door whispers, *come inside.*
Boy breathes, *it'll be okay.*

CITIES, TOWNS, AND TRAVEL

Poetry can take us from the quietest seaside town to the biggest, bustling city, on planes through the sky, over clickety train tracks, and on boats bobbing across the sea.

Map of Fun

Naomi Shihab Nye

Where did my feet walk today?
Did they step on a cloud, or into a sea?
Did a smooth wooden floor
welcome their beat?
They slid through the grass,
they stepped on a stone.
I dashed up the stairs.
My cat bit my toe.
I slid in the hall.
I splashed in a bath.
My fabulous feet felt it all.
Now they are curling under the sheet.
Tomorrow I will dance and run.
Skip and hop. Twirl and leap.
Feet always find the map of fun
and follow it.
But now, they rest,
they rest.

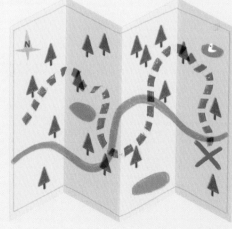

Direction

Alonzo Lopez

I was directed by my grandfather
To the East,
    so I might have the power of the bear;
To the South,
    so I might have the courage of the eagle;
To the West,
    so I might have the wisdom of the owl;
To the North,
    so I might have the craftiness of the fox;
To the Earth,
    so I might receive her fruit;
To the Sky,
    so I might lead a life of innocence.

If Once You Have Slept on an Island

Rachel Field

If once you have slept on an island
    You'll never be quite the same;
You may look as you looked the day before
    And go by the same old name,

You may bustle about in street and shop;
    You may sit at home and sew,
But you'll see blue water and wheeling gulls
    Wherever your feet may go.

You may chat with the neighbours of this and that
    And close to your fire keep,
But you'll hear ship whistle and lighthouse bell
    And tides beat through your sleep.

Oh, you won't know why, and you can't say how
 Such change upon you came,
But once you have slept on an island
 You'll never be quite the same!

First to See the Sea

Nicola Davies

Who will be the first to see the sea?
It will peek between the hills
or show a dreamy line beyond the highway.
Who will be first to feel their heart
fly up, and cry, "There! Oh, there!
There's the sea!" As if the whole ocean
had been lost, and found again.

Gran's Visit

Sally Murphy

Gran took me to the beach today.
The water washed my toes.
But when I felt a little scared
Gran smiled and kissed my nose.

Gran took me to the park today
And we played hide-and-seek.
But when I cried 'cause I felt lost
Gran smiled and kissed my cheek.

Gran had to pack her bag today
To go back to her place.
So when she looked a little sad
I smiled and kissed her face.

Peace by Piece

Celia Berrell

The world is getting smaller
and it's breaking into bits.
Let's put it back together
peace by piece
the puzzle fits.

Repairs can all be tended
by the tiniest of friends.
As working altogether
peace by piece
the puzzle mends.

Greetings

Lesléa Newman

I jumped aboard a midnight train.
I flew inside a silver plane.
I sailed a thirty-eight foot yacht,
I urged my horse into a trot,
I hitched my wagon to a star,
I drove a brand new racing car,
I took off in a shiny rocket,
I rode inside a giant's pocket.
I hailed a yellow taxi cab,
I crawled along beside a crab,
I slid downhill upon my skis,
I hopped across the tops of trees,
I climbed upon a wooly yak,
I held fast to a possum's back,
I came by subway, bus, and gnu,
Just to say hello to you.

City Rain

Rachel Field

Rain in the city!
  I love to see it fall
Slantwise where the buildings crowd
  Red brick and all.
Streets of shiny wetness
  Where the taxis go,
With people and umbrellas all
  Bobbing to and fro.

Rain in the city!
  I love to hear it drip
When I am cosy in my room
  Snug as any ship,
With toys spread on the table,
  With a picture book or two,
And the rain like a rumbling tune that sings
  Through everything I do.

City Lights

Lee Bennett Hopkins

Blazing lights

    flicker
    flash
    glitter
    gleam
    twinkle
    sparkle
    bedazzle
    beam

    so

    brilliantly
    bright.

Reasons
why
city
stays
awake
all
night.

City Home

Amy Ludwig VanDerwater

My city is bursting with treasures.
Pigeons peck crumbs in the rain.
The man on my corner sells flowers.
I travel to school on a train.

Musicians sing songs on the sidewalk.
Small children play ball in the park.
Listen. You'll hear every language.
It never gets lonely or dark.

I like when I visit the country.
It's neat to look up at the stars.
But I always miss these tall buildings.
And I miss the sound of the cars.

Stories

Allan De Fina

Only a city
has more stories
behind each windowed
shelf
than a library
can hold
or a storyteller
tell.

Skyscrapers

Rachel Field

Do skyscrapers ever grow tired
Of holding themselves up high?
Do they ever shiver on frosty nights
With their tops against the sky?

Do they feel lonely sometimes
Because they have grown so tall?
Do they ever wish they could lie right down
And never get up at all?

89

Dream Train

B.J. Lee

Trains echo through my dreams,
rumbling by in darkness
like faraway thunderstorms.
The train pushes a cone
of gold before it.
Sometimes the train stops
and I climb aboard.
I travel through the night
until I come to the place
where the dawn is born.
I walk in perfect sunlight,
then night comes again
and the train carries me home.

Rickety Train Ride

Tony Mitton

---

*(Rock backward and forward in time to the train rhythm,
or, for variety, from side to side.)*

I'm riding the train to Ricketywick.
Clickety clickety clack.
I'm sat in my seat
with a sandwich to eat
as I travel the trickety track.

It's an ever so rickety trickety train,
and I honestly thickety think
that before it arrives
at the end of the line
it will tip up my drippety drink.

Riding the Subway Train

Allan De Fina

Hurrying, hustling, hurtling past,
the subway train
approaches at last!

Whooshing, whizzing, whistling air,
blows in faces
and messes hair!

Rumble, rattle, screeching stop!
The train rolls in,
and on all hop.
Snap! Shut! Train doors close!
It jerks and lurches
as off it goes!

Whooshing, whizzing, whistling along!
The subway sings
its noisy song.

Canoe

Juanita Havill

Skimming through
liquid silver,
watch the surface
shimmer, shiver.
Stir the lake with a giant spoon
and glide across
the rippling moon.

Night Flight

Ted Scheu

Close your eyes
so we can fly
around the clouds,
across the sky.

Close your eyes
and hold on tight.
We'll zoom around
the moon tonight.

Close your eyes
and swoop with me
above the dark
and swirly sea.

Close your eyes
so dreams can soar
from pointy peak
to slippery shore.

And when we've been
from star to star,
from here to there,
from near to far,
from top to bottom,
coast to coast,
we'll float back home
for eggs and toast.

Traveling Together

Laura Purdie Salas

a plane of strangers
shares my grey metal feathers—
we become a bird

FUN AND GAMES

These poems put some of life's
simplest pleasures into words,
from riding a bike to flying a kite.

All Kinds of Kids

Elizabeth Steinglass

Hooray for the kids who love using words!
Hooray for the kids who chatter with birds!

Hooray for the kids who identify rocks!
Hooray for the kids who build bridges with blocks!

Hooray for the kids who sing to the stars!
Hooray for the kids who draw cats driving cars!

Hooray for the kids who count every stair!
Hooray for the kids who speak up for what's fair!

Hooray for all kinds of kids.

What do you do on a nature walk?

Kate Williams

We have an adventure, that's what –
crunching through the undergrowth,
dodging thorns and stings,
leaping logs and bridging bogs,
looking out for things:
birds and frogs and shy hedgehogs
and flies with fairy wings,
and slimy slugs and tiny bugs –
whatever nature brings!

Brothers

Peter Cole

Big
Strong
Billy
Matthews
Is
Very
Very
Tall,
Which
Makes
Him
Perfectly
Suited
For
Playing   Though his brother who is short
Basketball.   Is also good at sport.

What Can You Do with a Football?

James Carter

*Well.. you
can **kick it** you can
catch it you can **bounce it** all
around. You can **grab it** you can
pat it you can **roll it** on the ground.
You can **throw it** you can **head it** you
can **hit it** - with a bat. You can **biff
it** you can **boot it** you can **spin it**
you can **shoot it**. You can **drop
it** you can **stop it** - just
like that!*

Ice Skating

Sandra Liatsos

Higher and higher
I glide in the sky,
My feet flashing silver,
A star in each eye.
With wind at my back
I can float, I can soar.
The earth cannot hold me
In place anymore.

Tumbling

Anonymous

In jumping and tumbling
We spend the whole day,
Till night by arriving
Has finished our play.

What then? One and all,
There's no more to be said,
As we tumbled all day,
So we tumble to bed.

My Bike

Julie Larios

My bike is like a silver shark
swimming in the sea—
as fast as a shark, as fierce as a shark,
and no one can ride it but me.

Song of Kites

Anonymous

Our kite is rising in the sky
Playful winds will take it high.
Soaring, dancing higher yet
Up where clouds are floating by.

Falling, falling is the kite
Run and run to give it height.
See, our kite is rising now
Don't forget to hold on tight!

Note: This is a traditional rhyme from Japan.

Teammates

Elizabeth Steinglass

We stretch
together.
We run
together.
We dribble
together.
We kick
together.
We attack
together.
We defend
together.
We cheer
together.
We groan
together.
Together,
we meet
our fate.

Let's Go

Merry Bradshaw

Stretch High
Stretch Wide
Jump Forward
Jump Back

Lean Left
Lean Right
Hop Once
Hop Twice

Reach Up
Reach Down
Twist Small
Twist Tall

Shake Fast
Shake Slow
Touch Nose
Touch Toes

Stand Up
Let's Go!

My Shadow

Robert Louis Stevenson

I have a little shadow that goes in and out with me,
And what can be the use of him is more than I can see.
He is very, very like me from the heels up to the head;
And I see him jump before me, when I jump into my bed.

The funniest thing about him is the way he likes to grow—
Not at all like proper children, which is always very slow;
For he sometimes shoots up taller like an india-rubber ball,
And he sometimes gets so little that there's none of him at all.

He hasn't got a notion of how children ought to play,
And can only make a fool of me in every sort of way.
He stays so close beside me, he's a coward, you can see;
I'd think shame to stick to nursie as that shadow sticks to me!

One morning, very early, before the sun was up,
I rose and found the shining dew on every buttercup;
But my lazy little shadow, like an arrant sleepy-head,
Had stayed at home behind me and was fast asleep in bed.

A Circle of Sun

Rebecca Kai Dotlich

I'm dancing.

I'm leaping.

I'm skipping about.

I gallop.

I grin.

I giggle.

I shout.

I'm Earth's many colors,

I'm morning and night.

I'm honey on toast.

I'm bright.

I'm swinging.

I'm singing.

I wiggle.

I run.

I'm a piece of the sky

In a circle of sun.

What I Love About Summer

Douglas Florian

Morning glories
Campfire stories
Picking cherries
And blueberries
Riding bikes
Mountain hikes
Bird calls
Curve balls
Short sleeves
Green leaves
Swimming holes
Fishing poles
Nature walks
Corn stalks
Skipping stones
Ice cream cones
Double plays
And barefoot days.

Speak When This Way Talk Do I

Kenn Nesbitt

Speak when this way talk do I
so, if converse do we,
you'll talk to need to this way try
to talk with have a me.

It strange may somewhat first at sound
but for it try a bit.
It's this way fun I've talk to found.
I've done my life all it.

It's understand to hard know I
but and you'll try it see.
If sideways talk you can to try,
it's talk with fun to me.

The House of This Minute

Kate Coombs

I live in the house of this minute,
where all around me is real.
With freckles and giggles and wiggles,
with sun and rain to feel.

Come live with me in this minute!
We can race and shout and play—
for every day is this minute,
and this minute is every day.

I'm Much Too Tired to Play Tonight

Jack Prelutsky

I'm much too tired to play tonight,
I'm much too tired to talk,
I'm much too tired to pet the dog
or take him for a walk,
I'm much too tired to bounce a ball,
I'm much too tired to sing,
I'm much too tired to try to think
about a single thing.

I'm much too tired to laugh tonight,
I'm much too tired to smile,
I'm much too tired to watch TV
or read a little while,
I'm much too tired to drink my milk
or even nod my head,
but I'm not nearly tired enough
to have to go to bed.

I Can...

Tony Langham

Count to a hundred,
Read and write,
Draw a picture,
Fly a kite,
Rollerblade,
Do a handstand,
Play a tune
With an elastic band,
Swim a length,
Multiply,
Kick a football
Play I Spy,
Use a computer,
Tie my shoe,
I can do
Lots of things
– what about you?

Nobody's Birthday!

Marilyn Singer

It's nobody's birthday, but why should we wait?
There are thousands of things we can all celebrate.
Let's party for starfish and mushrooms and eagles.
Let's hoopla for hailstones and acorns and beagles.
Let's root for the grass and the whole Milky Way.
Let's cheer for the world each astonishing day.

unBIRTHDAY

Vikram Madan

Today is my unbirthday
It's your unbirthday too
Let's unexchange unpresents
Unhave an un-to-do

We'll unthrow an unparty
We'll unbake an uncake
We'll uninflate unballoons
Unclowns? No unmistake!

Unsmashing unpiñatas
Unrelishing untricks
Unordering unpizzas
Unwatching some unflicks

And when tomorrow turns up
We'll unstart un-anew
Tomorrow's my unbirthday
It's your unbirthday too!

SCIENCE AND ART

Poems can explore the scientific world,
raise searching questions, and show us how
to wonder, marvel, and be curious and creative.

NOW...

James Carter

The birth of a star.
The beat of a heart.

       The arc of an hour.
       The bee and the flower.

The flight of a swan.
The weight of the sun.

       A river in flood.
       The nature of blood.

The future in space
for this human race.

       Now that's
       what I call
       science

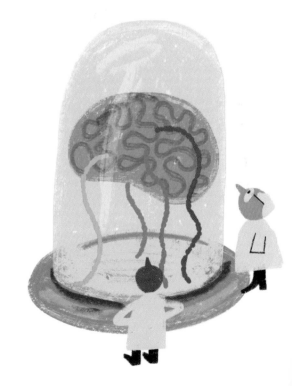

When You Are a Scientist

Eric Ode

When you are
a scientist,
ask what
and when
and how
and where
and why, why, why.

When you are
a scientist,
read,
and watch,
and think,
and write,
and try, try, try.

Da Vinci Did It!

Renée M. LaTulippe

In Italy, long, long ago,
a genius lived—
LEONARDO!

He was—
a painter, sculptor, mathematician,
engineer, and skilled musician

who dreamed up—
robots, carts, and parachutes,
flying planes and diving suits.

In fact—
as long as time did not forbid it,
you can bet da Vinci did it!

Fireworks

Celia Warren

Flames fly
Into the night,
Red and gold,
Effervescent and bright.
Watching children's
Oohs and Aahs, tell of
Rockets that zoom in
Kaleidoscope
Stars.

Our National Engineers Week

Suzy Levinson

Who designs a building that's
so tall it scrapes the sky?
And the airplanes high above ...
which seem too big to fly?

Who draws up the plans for stuff
like toasters and TVs?
How about computer chips,
bikes, and water skis?

Who creates things, big and small,
that we use every day?
The answer: engineers, of course!
This week's for them—hooray!

Questions That Matter

Heidi Bee Roemer

What is a solid?

"I am," says the wall.
"My size and shape remain the same;
I don't change at all."

What is a liquid?

"I am," says the milk.
"My carton gives me shape.
I'm a puddle when I'm spilt."

What is a gas?

"I am! Call me Steam-y!
My vapors fill the room,
but you probably can't see me."

Go Fly a Kite

Laura Purdie Salas

Above the kite, the pressure's low.
The air's a streaming, breezy flow.

Below the kite, the pressure's higher.
Up! Up! Up! This one's a fly-er!

Lift versus drag.
Lift wins!
That's why…

your kite
breaks
free
and
climbs
the
sky!

Testing My Magnet

Julie Larios

Flowers? No. Dirt? No.
Socks? No. Shirt? No.
Hamster? No. Snake? No.
Plastic scoop and rake? No.
Glue? Paint? Paper? Clay?
Sneakers that I wore today?
No, no, no, no…

Pile of metal paper clips—
Yes! Hooray for paper clips!
Shiny whistle? Metal fan?
Dented metal garbage can?
Hammer head, bag of nails?
Ring of keys? Rusty pails?
Yes, yes, yes, and yes!

Results of my experiment?
Magnets are mag-nificent!

Recycling

Susan Blackaby

Collect the daily scraps and clippings,
gather up the bits and snippings:
Paper, plastic, glass, and tin—
all of these go in the bin.
Once it's sorted and inspected,
so-called waste is redirected.
Think of all the things that you
can make from useful stuff you threw
away!

garbage

Valerie Worth

The stained,
Sour-scented
Bucket tips out
Hammered-gold
Orange rind

Eggshell ivory,
Garnet coffee-
Grounds, pearl
Wand of bared
Chicken bone:

Worked back soon
To still more
Curious jewelry
Of chemical
And molecule.

Old Water

April Halprin Wayland

I am having a soak in the tub.
Mom is giving my neck a strong scrub.

Water sloshes against the sides.
H_2O's seeping into my eyes.

The wet stuff running down my face?
She says it came from outer space!

The water washing between my toes
was born a billion years ago.

World Water Day

George Ella Lyon

See it flow: It's a river.
Stop it cold, and it's ice.
Watch it wave: It's the ocean
breaking once, breaking twice.

Water falls.
Water freezes.
Water mists,
and it pleases

oak and shark and butterfly
every thirsty thing that lives.
Next time you take a drink, think:
Life's the gift that water gives.

Note: World Water Day is held every year on March 22 to
focus on the importance of fresh water.

What Do the Trees Know?

Joyce Sidman

What do the trees know?

>To bend when all the wild winds blow.
>
>Roots are deep and time is slow.
>
>All we grasp we must let go.

What do the trees know?

>Buds can weather ice and snow.
>
>Dark gives way to sunlight's glow.
>
>Strength and stillness help us grow.

You Ask Why

Li Po

——

You ask why I make my home in the mountain forest,
and I smile, and am silent,
and even my soul remains quiet:
it lives in the other world
which no one owns.
The peach trees blossom.
The water flows.

Bluebirds

Jen Bryant

I built a house
of sturdy wood;
I waited and waited
as long as I could.

Then one sunny day
in the first week of May,
two bluebirds flew in
and decided to stay.

So I waited and waited
and waited some more,
now instead of just two
those bluebirds are FOUR!

Clay

Amy Ludwig VanDerwater

Hold a lump of clay.

What does it want to be?

Make a coil.

Pinch it.

Roll it.

Listen.

Set it free.

You will hear it tell you

what it is

what it is not.

And you will know

if you should shape

a puffin

or a pot.

My Colours

Colin West

These are
My colours,
One by one:

Red –
The poppies
Where I run.

Orange –
Summer's
Setting sun.

Yellow –
Farmers'
Fields of corn.

Green –
The clover
On my lawn.

Blue –
The sea
Where fishes spawn.

Indigo –
A starling's
Feather.

Violet –
The dancing
Heather.

A rainbow
They make
All together

Crayon Poem

James Carter

With these crayons
I could draw...

A crazy
purple dinosaur.

An *orange* mouse
with *yellow* cheese.

A big *black* dog
with big *brown* fleas.

A tall *blue* house,
a small *green* door
and four *white* windows.

Something more?

Silver raindrops.
Golden sun.

Then a ... *R A I N B O W*

sounds like fun!

Make a Joyful Noise

B.J. Lee

Pick on a banjo.
Bang on a drum.
What sound does it make?
Rum-tum-tum.

Shake some maracas.
Clack some sticks.
Grab your guitar
and play some licks.

Open your mouth
and sing a song,
or toot your kazoo
the whole day long.

Singing and Sashaying

Pat Mora

When I paint on white paper, I dip
my brush or fingertips and follow
the yellow and green swirls, suddenly see
a parrot on the paper looking at me.

When I sing, I sail
my song into the air,
hear a bird answer my yellow melody.
Inventing, we become a clever pair.

When I dance, my shoulder and
feet feel the beat. I spin, stamp,
try new rhythms as I sashay
      yellow steps down the leaf-covered street.

When I write, I listen,
hear stories and poems inside, repeat
sounds, play with colors and snappy beats.
      I create a great green parrot and me
          singing and sashaying down a yellow street.

BODY
AND HEALTH

In our everyday world, we eat and drink, rest and grow,
wash and sleep. Poems can make these mundane activities
seem interesting, unusual, and even hilarious.

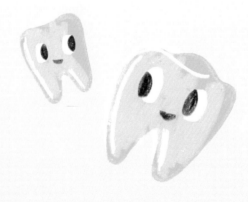

My Corner

Cheryl Moskowitz

I have a corner where I go
A place that no one really knows
It's where I sit to have my thoughts
And plan my life out, I suppose

It's quite a quiet little spot
As quiet goes, it's all I've got
When people ask me where I've been
Don't know if I should tell or not

There are lots of other kids I've seen
(Who need that sort of space, I mean)
But in this place I'm all alone
So I'm not telling anything

Though I don't have a bed or phone
My corner's like a little home
That I'll remember when I've grown
That I'll remember when I've grown

Summer

Walter Dean Myers

I like hot days, hot days
Sweat is what you got days
Bugs buzzin from cousin to cousin
Juices dripping
Running and ripping
Catch the one you love days

Birds peeping
Old men sleeping
Lazy days, daisies lay
Beaming and dreaming
Of hot days, hot days,
Sweat is what you got days

Trudging

Anonymous

The night was growing old
    As she trudged through snow and sleet;
And her nose was long and cold,
    And her shoes were full of feet.

Just a Skin Thing

Coral Rumble

This is the skin
That I've grown up in.
I've filled every part
And look pretty smart.
It starts at my head,
Reaches down to my feet,
It stretches so I can
Sit down on a seat.
It's got a few freckles
That others can see,
And finger print markings
To prove that I'm me.
Skin comes in all sizes
And colours and shades,
And proves, without doubt,
We're all brilliantly made!

Bath Time

Eric Ode

A scrubbly, bubbly,
Rub-a-dub jumble.
A slippery, drippery slosh.
A muddle, a puddle,
A tumbly tuddle.
A jiggly, wriggly wash.

A splattery swish,
A splosh and a splish.
A drippy and flippery flash.
A bath full of bubble.
A tub full of trouble.
A wiggle, a giggle,
Kersplash!

Bubbles

Jacqueline Jules

———————

Wiggle the soap!
Make some bubbles!
Wash away
germs and troubles.

Twenty seconds
is all it takes
to chase away
a stomachache.

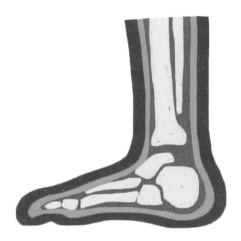

What Is a Foot?

Jane Yolen

You will find a foot at the end of your limb,

Where you might wear a fin when you go for a swim.

It's got segments galore, it's got bones by the dozens,

And the bones have more bones, who are all sort of cousins.

As for animal feet, there's a soft foot, or paw,

That ends in strong nails, and is often called claw.

But others have hard feet, a hoof as we say.

And that is a feat of foot facts for today.

barefoot

Valerie Worth

After that tight
Choke of sock
And blunt
Weight of shoe,

The foot can feel
Clover's green
Skin
Growing,

And the fine
Invisible
Teeth
Of gentle grass,

And the cool
Breath
Of the earth
Beneath.

I Sit On My Bottom

Michael Salinger

I sit on my bottom
I stand on my feet
My belly gets
The food that I eat
My eyes see the world
My hands reach and grab
My knees bend and jump
My mouth likes to gab
My heart pumps my blood
My lungs breathe in air
My brain makes things run
I have a liver somewhere
All these bits and pieces
Even some you can't see
All linked up together
Are what make up ... me.

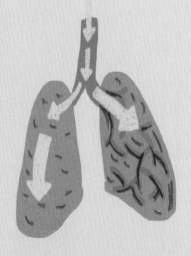

Catching a Yawn

Avis Harley

Why is it I'm always drawn
into someone else's yawn?

Every time I see the shape
of open mouth in cave-like gape
l feel the need to do the same,
as if it's some contagious game.

Perhaps it's empathy that stirs
when someone else's yawn occurs.

But even seeing the word in print
will send my brain the strongest hint
that I must yawn. And so I do.
Did reading this make you yawn, too?

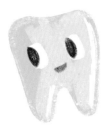

Loose Tooth, Whose Tooth?

Carole Boston Weatherford

Loose tooth, whose tooth?
Bat's tooth, rat's tooth.
Loose tooth, whose tooth?
Snail's tooth, whale's tooth.
Loose tooth, whose tooth?
Aardvark's tooth, shark's tooth.
Loose tooth, whose tooth?
Shrew's tooth, gnu's tooth.
Loose tooth, whose tooth?
Gorilla's tooth, chinchilla's tooth.
Loose tooth, whose tooth?
Piranha's tooth, iguana's tooth.
Loose tooth, whose tooth?
Boar's tooth, your tooth.

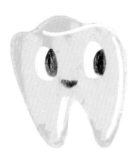

Tooth

Amy Ludwig VanDerwater

Wiggle.
Wiggle.

Bite.
Bite.

I will pull
it out

tonight!

Grandfather's Chopsticks

Janet Wong

Grandfather's chopsticks
are like extra-long
superhero fingers,
able to grab anything
on the big round
restaurant table.

He picks up
a piece of my favorite
honey walnut shrimp
and puts it on my plate.
Slippery noodles.
Fried chicken—
crispy skin
and tender white meat.

Grandfather's chopsticks
are pretty smart:
how do they know
exactly
what I want to eat?

Global Gorging

Terry Webb Harshman

New York bagels!
Scottish scones!
Warm, Italian
cheese calzones!

Irish soda bread
with stew!
Crusty French bread!
Croissants, too!

Chinese dumplings!
Egg rolls, noodles!
English muffins!
German strudels!

Seeded, twisted,
Flat or curled—
I'll eat my way
AROUND THE WORLD!

Breakfast

Linda Sue Park

For this meal, people like what they like, the same every morning.
Toast and coffee, Bagel and juice. Cornflakes and milk in a white bowl.

Or—warm, soft, and delicious—a few extra minutes in bed.

I Eat My Peas with Honey

Anonymous

I eat my peas with honey;
I've done it all my life.
It makes the peas taste funny,
But it keeps them on the knife.

A Dream Without Hunger

Michael J. Rosen

Imagine the day—how else
can change begin?—when no one

goes to bed hungry
and no one rises hungry.

Imagine that dawn
when all of us awaken

from hunger's nightmare
and breakfast is no dream.

Imagine such a day.
It can't be far away.

To Yahola, On His First Birthday

Alexander Posey

The sky has put her bluest garment on,
    And gently brushed the snowy clouds away;
The robin trills a sweeter melody,
    Because you are just one year old today.

The wind remembers, in his sweet refrains,
    Away, away up in the tossing trees,
That you came in the world a year ago,
    And earth is filled with pleasant harmonies,

        And all things seem to say,
        "Just one year old today."

Growing

Tony Mitton

Today
you may be small.
But one day
you'll be tall,
like me,
maybe taller.
You won't
fit into your bed.
Your hat
won't fit on your head.
Your feet will fill up the floor.
You'll have to bend down
to come through the door.
You'll be able to reach
on the highest shelf,
(and I can't do that now,
myself).

Out in the country
the tallest trees
will scratch your ankles
and tickle your knees.
Up in the clouds,
yes, way up there,
the eagles will nest
in your craggy hair.
But they'd better soon find
a safer place
because soon your head
will be up in space.

So I hope you won't be too proud
to bend down
and say hello
to your old home-town.
And I hope it won't drive you
utterly mad
to visit your tiny
Mum and Dad.

Winter Counting

Joseph Bruchac

How many winters
do you have?
That's how we ask
someone their age.

The snow that fell,
then melted away,
reminds us that
we still are here.

It's easy to count
your age by years.
We think winter counting
is a better way.

It makes us grateful
for the spring
when every bird
and every flower
welcomes us to
a whole new time.

Then sunshine is
in every heart
and we smile
as we ask each other
how many winters
do you have now?

A WORLD OF LEARNING

Reading, thinking, and studying keep our minds active and help us grow as people. Poets have captured the moments of joy, surprise, and even frustration that learning brings in fresh and interesting ways.

Mrs Kenning

Paul Cookson

Loud shouter
Deep thinker
Rain hater
Coffee drinker

Spell checker
Sum ticker
Line giver
Nit picker

Ready listener
Trouble carer
Hometime lover
Knowledge sharer

Underwear Scare

Terry Webb Harshman

I got off the bus
and found my room.
I found my desk
    and chair.

Then suddenly
my teacher said,
"You're in your
    underwear!"

Down the hallway
I ran
    SCREAMING!

Thank goodness I
was only
    dreaming.

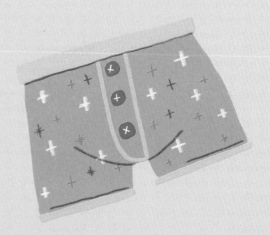

Sophie

Steven Herrick

It's like I thought it would be.
Absolute silence.
Just me and my poem.
But,
as I stand onstage
preparing to start,
I realize the audience is quiet
because they want to hear me.
Silence isn't scary.
It's like Mr. Carey said,
silence is my chance.
And so I speak,
slowly
and clearly,
and I don't see
the faces in front of me.
I see the images of my poem,
and I think only of what I'm saying
and how much it means to me.
My voice grows stronger
and I don't have to struggle
to remember the words.

I know them
because I wrote them.

My Needs

JonArno Lawson

I need a little time to squander

A book to read

A place to wander

And puzzling quandaries I can ponder.

Homework!
Oh, Homework!

Jack Prelutsky

Homework! Oh, Homework!
I hate you! You stink!
I wish I could wash you
away in the sink,
if only a bomb
would explode you to bits.
Homework! Oh, Homework!
You're giving me fits.

I'd rather take baths
with a man-eating shark,
or wrestle a lion
alone in the dark,
eat spinach and liver,
pet ten porcupines,
than tackle the homework
my teacher assigns.

Homework! Oh, Homework!
you're last on my list,
I simply can't see
why you even exist,
if you disappeared
it would tickle me pink.
Homework! Oh, Homework!
I hate you! You stink!

Time

Mary Ann Hoberman

Listen to the clock strike
One
    two
        three,
Up in the tall tower
One
    two
        three.
Hear the hours slowly chime;
Watch the hands descend and climb;
Listen to the sound of time
One
    two
        three.

Nature Knows Its Math

Joan Graham

Divide
the year
into seasons,
four,
subtract
the snow then
add
some more
green,
a bud,
a breeze,
a whispering
behind
the trees,
and here
beneath the
rain-scrubbed
sky
orange poppies
multiply.

Bilingual

Alma Flor Ada

Because I speak Spanish
I can listen to my grandmother's stories
and say *familia, madre, amor.*
Because I speak English
I can learn from my teacher
and say **I love school.**
Because I am bilingual
I can read *libros* and **books,**
I have *amigos* and **friends,**
enjoy *canciones* and **songs,**
juegos and **games**
and have twice as much fun.
And someday,
because I speak two languages,
I will be able to do twice as much
to help twice as many people
and be twice as good in what I do.

One to Ten

Janet Wong

Yut yee sam see
Count in Cantonese with me!

Eun look chut bot
Can you tell me what we've got?

Gow sup. One to ten!
(Could you say that once again?)

Ratty Writing

James Aitchison

Slopy loops,

O's like hoops,

b's like d's,

a's like e's,

are they m's?

are they n's?

c that e?

no, it's c,

lots of blots,

lots of dots —

what a scrawl,

can't read at all!

Good Books, Good Times!

Lee Bennett Hopkins

Good books.
Good times.
Good stories.
Good rhymes.
Good beginnings.
Good ends.
Good people.
Good friends.
Good fiction.
Good facts.
Good adventures.
Good acts.
Good stories.
Good rhymes.
Good books.
Good times.

The Library

Sara Holbrook

Take the walk
to the open door,
this is where you
find out more
about the stars,
oceans, quakes,
dragons, cars,
cheetahs, snakes,
unicorns, and
jumping beans,
horses, bugs,
and time machines.
From killer whales,
and free-tailed bats,
to hammer heads
and kitty cats,
the library has got a book.
Come on in,
take a look.

Learn how to cook
or write a poem.
Read it here
or take it home.
What do you want to learn about?
It's free!
It's here!
Check it out!

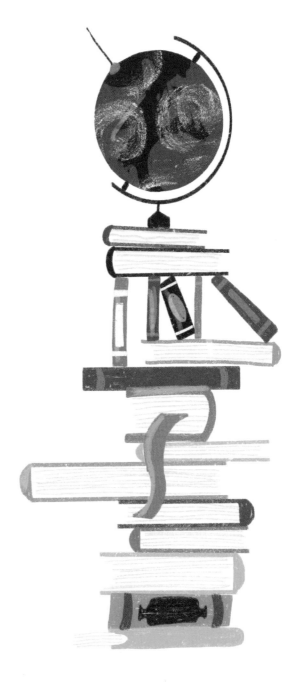

Stop! Let's Read

Kristy Dempsey

Wherever you are,
it's time to stop!
Grab a book
and find a spot.
Look at pictures,
see new faces,
word by word,
discover places.
You say: *Read!*
and I'll join in.
Ready, set,
just begin…
Let's start slow
and pick up speed.
Hey, everyone!
It's time to read!

So I Picked Out a Book

Karla Kuskin

So I picked out a book
on my own
from the shelf
and I started to read
on my own
to myself.
And nonsense and knowledge
came tumbling out,
whispering mysteries,
history's shout,
the wisdom of wizards,
the songs of the ages,
all wonders of wandering
wonderful pages.

Secret Worlds

Margarita Engle

Please don't worry or fret today.
Just enjoy one page at a time.
Read a story, or poems that rhyme.
Write if you have something to say.

Each book is like a passageway
to secret worlds where you can play.

Reading will take you far away
to mountain peaks that you can climb
or dark swamps filled with thick green slime.
(Read backwards if you lose your way!)

Note: This poem is in the style of a Cuban *décima* mirror. It has two stanzas of four lines, with eight syllables each and a rhyming pattern, with a bridge in between.

Dive into a Book

J.R. Poulter

I took a peak.
It looked so cool,
I dived right in
The wordage pool!

It was deep
And it was wide!
A whole world
Opened up inside...

I'm all immersed
In wondrous lands!
I'm getting versed
In plots and plans!

I think I'm getting
In the swim!
Why don't you come
And dive right in?!

Surprise

Beverly McLoughland

The biggest
Surprise
On the library shelf
Is when you suddenly
Find yourself
Inside a book—
(The *hidden* you).

You wonder how
The author knew.

My Book!

David L. Harrison

I did it!
I did it!

Come and look
At what I've done!
I read a book!
When someone wrote it
Long ago
For me to read,
How did he know
That this was the book
I'd take from the shelf
And lie on the floor
And read by myself?
I really read it!
Just like that!
Word by word,
From first to last!
I'm sleeping with
This book in bed,
This first FIRST book
I've ever read!

POETRY
ACTIVITIES

Sharing your favorite poems with friends and family is lots of fun. It may even inspire you to write your own poems! The tips and ideas in this section will help you do both.

Reading aloud

A great reading can bring a poem to life.

Be sure to begin by saying the title and author of the poem.

Pronounce each word clearly and distinctly.

Pause at the end of lines and when you see commas or periods.

Look at your audience whenever you can.

Use a portable microphone for fun if you have one—or pretend with a spoon or a hairbrush!

Acting it out

Here are some more creative ideas for sharing a poem in dramatic ways that will make it memorable.

Use simple props, such as puppets, when reading your poem out loud.

Add movements or pantomime while you read.

Play music in the background to create a special mood.

Use sound effects to liven up your reading.

Translate your favorite poem into another language if you can. Ask a friend or family member who speaks the language to help.

Poem treasure hunt

See if you can find one poem in this book for each of the following clues. Hunt with a friend if you like.

1
Find a poem that rhymes.

2
Find a poem that does NOT rhyme.

3
Find a poem with words that are NOT English words.

4
Find a poem that's about the weather.

5
Find a poem that would be fun to read for someone's birthday.

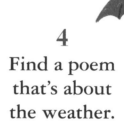

6
Find a poem that mentions a color.

7
Find a poem that's fewer than 10 lines long.

What did you notice about this poem?

What's your favorite line or word in the poem?

Sharing opinions

Talking about a poem with other people might help you understand different points of view, or even change what you think of the poem yourself. Here are some questions you could use to start a conversation.

Does the poem remind you of anything?

What's the feeling you get from reading or listening to this poem?

What makes this poem a poem?

Starting to write

2

Collect words
for your poems that
make you stop and
think. Poets use as
few words as possible
and choose each
one carefully.

3

Copy out a
favorite poem to
get a feel for how it
works. Could you
write something in
the same style?

1

Reading is the
best way to become
a poet! So read as
many poems as you
can—it will help you
write your own.

If you would like to
try writing your
own poems,
here are some
easy tips for
getting started.

4

Now write a poem in
whatever way you like.
Then change ONE line
or word in it. This helps
you think about your
idea in a different way.

5

Finally, read your
poem aloud to a friend
or your family. Their
feedback will help you
improve. Now write
some more poems!

Next steps

Once you've begun writing poems, write LOTS of them. Some will be wonderful and others you'll forget. Here are some techniques to try.

Write a poem that rhymes. You can use rhyme at the end of the lines, in the middle, or just occasionally.

Try writing a poem that repeats a word or a line more than once to emphasize it.

Experiment with free verse. You could try to develop a rhythm, but don't worry about rhyme.

Try writing a poem that has a simile, by using "like" or "as" to describe or compare something with something you might not expect.

Use alliteration to repeat the same consonant sound at the beginning of many words for emphasis.

Styles to try

Once you've started writing poems of your own, you might want to experiment with different styles. Here are some to try out.

List poem

A simple list of things that go together can make a poem, with an opening and closing to complete it. A list poem does not usually rhyme, and it sometimes ends with a surprise! (See **"How to Love Your Little Corner of the World"** by **Eileen Spinelli** on page 51.)

Question poem

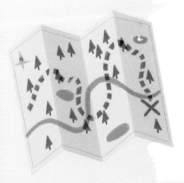

This style of poem asks a question or includes a question in each line. The questions are usually connected in some way, and it also has opening and closing lines to tie it all together. (See **"Map of Fun"** by **Naomi Shihab Nye** on page 78.)

Shape poem

If you're clever, you can arrange the words and lines of your poem so that they make a shape that matches the topic. (See **"What Can You Do with a Football?"** by **James Carter** on page 101.)

Haiku
This traditional Japanese poem has three lines
and is usually about the natural world. The first
and third lines each have five syllables and the
second line has seven.
(See **"Traveling Together"** by **Laura Purdie Salas** on page 95.)

Sijo
This Korean type of poem has three
lines with 14 to 16 syllables in each line,
making a total of 42 to 48 syllables.
(See **"Breakfast"** by **Linda Sue Park** on page 158.)

Written a poem?

There are many
ways to share a poem
with friends—by mail,
phone, text, email,
or video, as well as
face-to-face.

Now share it!

Turn your poem into art

Sometimes it's fun to add art to your writing or turn your poem into an artwork. Try one of these ideas.

Make your poem into a greeting card. Write the poem inside the card, and add your own drawing on the front to illustrate it.

Turn your poem into a 3-D model! Write it on pieces of card stock, and then use string and sticks or rods to make a mobile.

Get digital! Use a computer to create a collage or poster featuring your poem, adding images you like.

Decorate your fridge. Write the words of a short poem on individual magnetic labels. Rearrange the words on the fridge to make new poems!

Use your poem to make a gift for a loved one. Write it on special paper, add a painting or drawing, and put it in a frame.

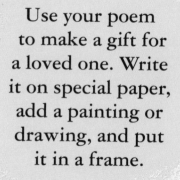

Getting better as a poet

Seeing your writing with a clear eye and noticing ways to improve it are useful skills. Asking yourself these questions may help.

What doesn't make sense or isn't
clear in my poem when I hear myself
read it out loud?

Should I add something more to
my poem to make it clearer or
more interesting?

Are there any words or even lines
in my poem that I don't need?
What should I cut?

How does my poem look on the page?
How do I want it to look?

Do I like the way my poem begins?
Am I happy with how it ends? What
should I change or rearrange?

A day full of poems

Here are some ideas to add poetry to your daily life.

Start the day with a poem at breakfast.

If your family has a car, keep a book of poetry inside it to read on car trips.

Copy out a poem and keep it in your backpack.

Search for poems on your cell phone or tablet.

Write a poem about someone you admire.

Write a poem
on the sidewalk
with chalk.

Turn your
favorite poem
into the lyrics
of a song.

Record a poem to share
with a friend or family
member far away.

Learn a poem by heart
to impress a friend on
a special occasion.

Look in your school
library for poetry
books to read.

End the day
with a poem
at dinner
or bedtime.

GLOSSARY

acrostic poem
Poem in which the first letter of the first word in every line spells out a word or a phrase downward that is usually the theme of the poem

alliteration
When a poet uses words beginning with the same consonant several times in a row

couplet
Pair of lines or verses that usually rhyme

free verse
Poems that do not rhyme, do not have a regular rhythm, and may have lines of different lengths

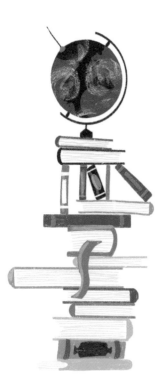

haiku
Traditional, three-line Japanese poem that is usually about the natural world. The first and third lines each contain five syllables, and the second line has seven

imagery
When a poet uses words that involve the senses—sight, hearing, smell, touch, and so on—to paint a picture in the reader's mind

limerick
Funny poem that has five lines. The first, second, and last lines rhyme, as do the shorter third and fourth lines

list poem
Poem with a list of things that go together, enclosed by an opening and ending. It does not usually rhyme and sometimes ends with a surprise. Also called a litany poem

lyrical poem
Usually a short poem that expresses the poet's emotions from a first-person ("I") point of view

metaphor
Comparison of one thing or idea to another in an indirect or hidden way

meter
Pattern of words and syllables in a poem creating a distinctive rhythm or beat and a musical sound

narrative poem
Poem that tells a story with a beginning, middle, and end, sometimes rhyming and sometimes in free verse

onomatopoeia
When poets use sounds and sound words, such as "buzz," "whoosh," and "zing," to make their poems more interesting, especially for reading aloud

personification
Imagining what something that is not human might be like if it had human feelings or experiences

quatrain
Verse with four lines that usually rhyme

repetition
Reusing, or repeating, a word or line in a poem to give it more emphasis or importance

rhyme
Effect in which words or syllables at the ends of lines—and sometimes in the middle—sound the same

rhythm
Regular pattern of beats and breaths in a line of poetry that gives the reader a feeling of movement or sound

shape poem
Poem in which all the words and lines are arranged in the shape of the poem's theme. Also called a concrete poem

sijo
Traditional Korean poem that has three lines with 14 to 16 syllables in each line, making a total of 42 to 48 syllables

simile
Comparison between two things or ideas, usually using "as" or "like"

stanza
Group of lines, also called a verse, in a poem, often in a regular pattern

syllable
Unit of pronunciation made up of a vowel sound with or without consonants. It may be a whole word or part of one

tercet
Stanza of three lines that often incorporates rhyme

200

INDEX

POETS

POEMS

TOPICS

Acknowledgments

The publisher would like to thank the following people for their assistance in the preparation of this book: Kathleen Teece and Katie Lawrence for editorial assistance; Caroline Hunt for proofreading; and Radhika Haswani for compiling the poetry credits.

Sylvia Vardell would like to thank her family for their constant support, especially Russell; her friend and poetry collaborator, Janet Wong; her guide for this project, Abby Aitcheson; and all the poets who shared their gifts, especially Lee Bennett Hopkins.